Something to enjoy
along with the wonderful
miracle who arrived in
your lives this morning.
Love,
Mom

IN
CELEBRATION
OF BABIES

D0879176

IN
CELEBRATION
OF BABIES

Selections by
Carol Tannenhauser
and
Cheryl Moch

Fawcett Columbine · New York

To those who gave us life

and those who give it meaning

A Fawcett Columbine Book
Published by Ballantine Books

Due to limitations of space, permissions acknowledgments for text and illustrations may be found at the back of this book.

Library of Congress Catalog Card Number: 90-82334

ISBN 0-449-90565-9

Cover design by James R. Harris
Cover illustration by Marika Hahn

Manufactured in the United States of America

First Trade Edition: May 1991

10 9 8 7 6 5 4 3 2 1

CHAPTERS

INTRODUCTION

What happens when a mother of two, wondering if babies are in her past, and a single woman, wondering if they are in her future, join together to create a "sweet little collection" of quotations and art, "in celebration of babies"?

What happens after months of meeting in the New York Public Library, rediscovering—or savoring for the first time—the greatest writers of all time, men and women, on one theme: babies? Moving from section to section in search of diversity and balance: a day of poetry, another of humor; a morning of women's fiction, a night of lullabies. Essays, journals, autobiographies, child-care manuals, the Bible, popular music; what happens after exposure to so many different perspectives, approaches, and points of view?

And what happens after months of searching through photo libraries; advertising, greeting-card, and magazine archives; galleries and exhibitions; museum catalogues and art books; becoming experts at "finding the baby." Watching anxious photographers, with oversized portfolios, flip through picture after picture—hundreds of pictures—of babies being born, at the breast, in the bath, sleeping, smiling, crying, crawling, walking away; finding the perfect image, then a more perfect image, finally, begging each other to stop.

It's been a time of endless surprises; bits of wisdom and clarity on scraps of paper; phone calls ("I just have to read you this one . . ."); and, above all, discovery; the Norman Rockwell in a tiny antique shop; the cousin whose poetry—shyly handed over at a holiday dinner—held its own beside the greats; the endless stream of brown cardboard envelopes, arriving by parcel post, eagerly opened to reveal the latest batch of possibilities; the personal favorites: that baby's incredible eyes; the way that poem works with that picture; the quirky old ballad; the "hunky guy" tenderly cradling his newborn son.

Inevitably, the sweet little collection became much more: a dialogue representing the full range of thoughts and feelings—good and bad—that come with a baby; a chronicle—eloquent and visual—of the beginning of life and love. Perhaps most striking of all was the universality of the experience; words and images began to blur into one voice, one family, one baby, confirming what Carl Sandburg wrote: "There is only one child in the world and the child's name is All Children."

What happens when such a wonderful project ends? The mother of two and the single woman are now fast friends, with a sense of having glimpsed each other's inner vision and agreed, currently seeking something new to celebrate. As for babies, we are both still wondering.

Carol Tannenhauser · Cheryl Moch   *New York City*

FOREWORD

Well, as Margaret Mead would have said, "Piffle." Piffle to the human conceit of rational childbearing. Reason may determine the timing of children and the number of children, but I think it has less to do with the decision to have a baby . . . than with the decision to fall in love . . .

Reason advises people to reduce the risks of their life. Reason is cautious in the face of change. Reason cannot really imagine the depths of feeling and connection that come with childbirth, the way in which the palette of human emotions opens up from primary colors to a vast and subtle rainbow. Reason can only think of diapers.

Ellen Goodman from "A Celebration of the Emotions" in *Close to Home*

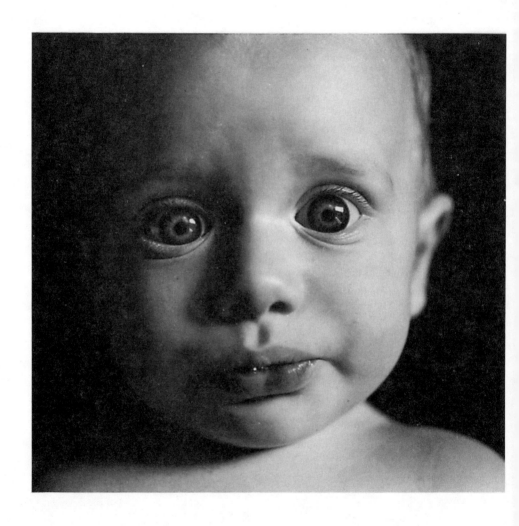

BEGINNINGS

Something to live for came to the place,

Something to die for maybe,

Something to give even sorrow a grace,

And yet it was only a baby!

Harriet Prescott Spofford from "Only"

Where did you come from, Baby dear?
Out of the everywhere into here.

Where did you get your eyes so blue?
Out of the sky as I came through.

What makes the light in them sparkle and spin?
Some of the starry spikes left in.

Where did you get that little tear?
I found it waiting when I got here.

What makes your forehead so smooth and high?
A soft hand stroked it as I went by.

What makes your cheek like a warm white rose?
I saw something better than anyone knows.

George MacDonald from "Baby"

Little Lamb, who made thee?
Dost thou know who made thee?
Gave thee life, & bid thee feed,
By the stream & o'er the mead;
Gave thee clothing of delight,
Softest clothing, wooly, bright;
Gave thee such a tender voice,
Making all the vales rejoice?

William Blake from "The Lamb"

Our birth is but a sleep and a forgetting:

The Soul that rises with us, our life's Star,

    Hath had elsewhere its setting,

    And cometh from afar;

    Not in entire forgetfulness,

    And not in utter nakedness,

But trailing clouds of glory do we come

From God, who is our home:

Heaven lies about us in our infancy!

William Wordsworth from "Ode, Intimations of Immortality from Recollections of Early Childhood"

Sometimes I can almost see, around our heads,

like gnats around a streetlight in summer,

the children we could have,

the glimmer of them.

Sometimes I feel them waiting, dozing

in some antechamber—servants, half—

listening for the bell.

Sometimes I see them lying like love letters

in the Dead Letter Office.

And sometimes, like tonight, by some black

second sight I can feel just one of them

standing on the edge of a cliff by the sea

in the dark, stretching its arms out

desperately to me.

Sharon Olds "The Unborn"

When the moon shines on the sea

I see the babies

riding on the moonwaves

asking to be born.

Erica Jong from "Playing With the Boys"

A man deposits seed in a womb and goes away, and then another

cause takes it, and labors on it, and makes a baby.

What a consummation from such a beginning!

Marcus Aurelius from "Meditations"

Frail newborn wings,

Small voice that sings,

New little beating heart,

Dread not thy birth,

Nor fear the earth—

The Infinite thou art.

The sun doth shine

The earth doth spin,

For welcome—enter in

This green and daisied sphere,

Rejoice—and have no fear.

Richard LeGallienne

Mrs. Tracy was growing a baby. She fed the baby very carefully.

For breakfast she gave the baby milk, soft-boiled eggs, and good raisin toast.

"Do you like your food?" she asked.

And from deep inside her, Baby would say, "Ummm."

After breakfast, Mrs. Tracy would go into a sunny room and paint.

She would put red, blue, and every other color

on paper and paint them into lovely shapes. Then she would tell

Baby about them. "Do you like your pictures?" she asked.

And Baby would say, "Ummm." The days went by pleasantly,

until one day when Mrs. Tracy took Baby for a walk in the woods.

"Baby, there are so many little yellow flowers. When you are born,

you will see them for yourself." " I don't want to be born," said Baby.

"Oh yes, you must be born!" said Mrs. Tracy.

"I am staying right here," insisted Baby. Mrs. Tracy started to cry.

Fran Manushkin from *Baby, Come Out!*

Our birth is nothing but our death begun.

Edward Young from "Night Thoughts"

The baby is closely confined in a warm dark prison of exquisite, neutral comfort.
Everything around him is of the same texture
and at the same temperature as himself.
. . . amniotic fluid fills the spaces between his body and the walls of the womb;
there is no friction, no sensation, no change. His eyes are ready but
there is nothing for him to see. . . . He has no need to breathe nor
does he need to digest food, so he feels no sensations from
within himself. He can sense sound and movement,
but even they are muffled by his insulated liquid environment.
He is sealed off from the world, untouched and untouchable.

Penelope Leach *Your Baby & Child*

How luxurious, pregnancy!
a perfect universe mine
to offer.

Susan Eisenberg from "Offerings, for Zoe Margaret"

Be fruitful, and multiply . . .

Genesis

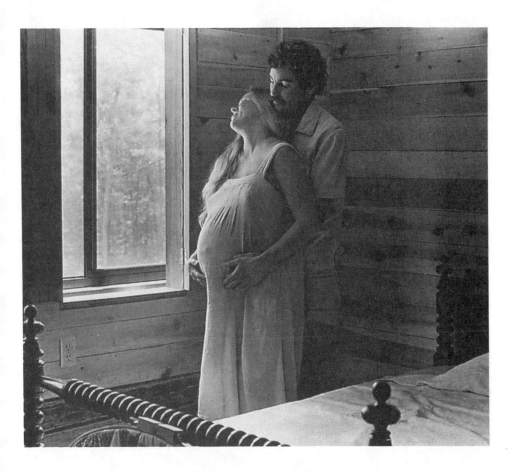

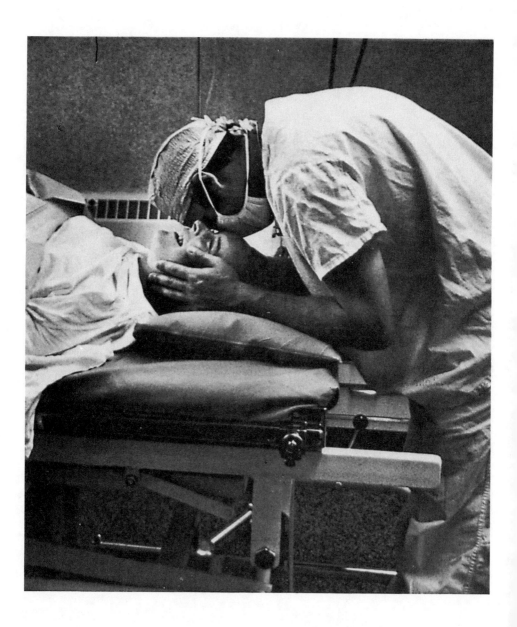

BIRTH

An intransigent force—wild, out of control—has gripped the infant.

A blind force that hammers at it and impels it downward . . .

Overpowered, it huddles up as tightly as it can. With its head tucked in

and its shoulders hunched together, it is hardly more than a little ball of fright.

The prison has gone berserk, demanding its prisoner's death. The walls

close in still further. The cell becomes a passageway; the passage, a tunnel.

With its heart bursting, the infant sinks into this hell.

Its fear is without limit.

Frederick Leboyer *Birth Without Violence*

My mother groan'd, my father wept,
Into the dangerous world I leapt:
Helpless, naked, piping loud,
Like a fiend hid in a cloud.

William Blake from "Infant Sorrow"

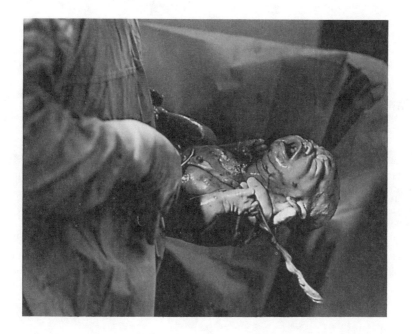

The universe resounds with the joyful cry I am.

Scriabin

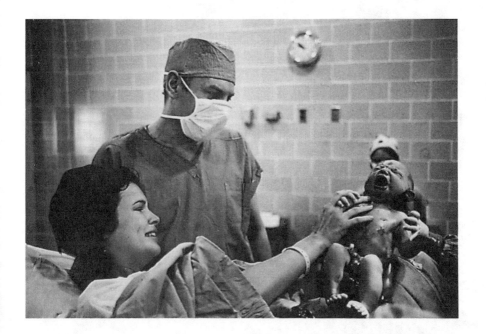

Congratulations! Life as you know it is over.

Contemporary greeting card

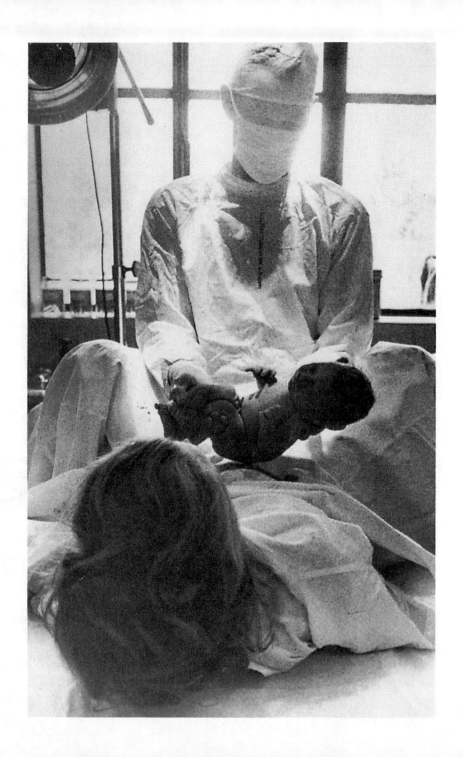

FIRST
IMPRESSIONS

Ah, what an incomparable thrill. All that heaving, the amazing damp
slippery wetness and hotness, the confused sight of dark gray ropes of cord,
the blood, the baby's cry. The sheer pleasure of the feeling
of a born baby on one's thighs is like nothing on earth.

Margaret Drabble *With All My Love, (Signed) Mama*

Babies are bits of star-dust blown from the hand of God. Lucky the woman who
knows the pangs of birth for she has held a star.

Larry Barretto *The Indiscreet Years*

God one morning, glad of heaven,
Laughed—and that was you!

Brian Hooker from "A Little Person"

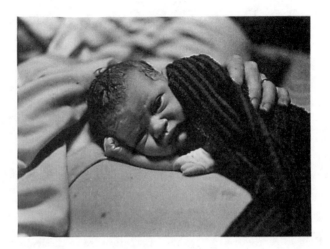

A sweet, new blossom of Humanity,

Fresh fallen from God's own home to flower

on earth.

Gerald Massey from "Wooed and Won"

. . . the baby came out, and my wife and I were suddenly sharing the greatest
moment in our lives. This was what we had asked God for; this was what we
wanted to see if we could make. And I looked at it lovingly as they started
to clean it off, but it wasn't getting any better.

And then I went over to my wife, kissed her gently on the
lips, and said, "Darling, I love you very much. You just had a lizard."

Bill Cosby *Fatherhood*

All God's children are not beautiful.

Most of God's children are, in fact, barely presentable.

Fran Liebowitz *Metropolitan Life*

Mountains will heave in childbirth, and a silly little mouse will be born.

Horace from "Ars. Poetica"

When I was born, I drew in the common air, and fell upon the earth . . .

and the first voice which I uttered was crying, as all others do. . . .

For there is no king that had any other beginning of birth . . .

all men have one entrance into life, and the like going out.

Wisdom of Solomon

The first cry of a newborn baby in Chicago or Zamboango,
in Amsterdam or Rangoon, has the same pitch and key, each saying, "I am!
I have come through! I belong! I am a member of the Family."

Carl Sandburg from the "Prologue" to *The Family of Man*

Babies are unreasonable; they expect far too much of existence.
Each new generation that comes takes one look at the world, thinks wildly,
"Is this all they've done to it?" and bursts into tears.

Clarence Day *The Crow's Nest*

When they first brought the baby in to her . . .
she stared, inert, and thought, This is the author of my pain.

Bessie Breuer *The Actress*

Every baby born into the world is a finer one than the last.

Charles Dickens *Nicholas Nickleby*

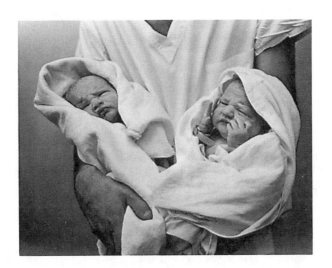

. . . a baby boy, ain't it great, Hat?

W.C. Fields Letter to his wife Hattie

It's a girl . . . a little beauty, an angel, and I'm madly in love with her.

Henry Miller On the birth of his daughter

Small traveler from an unseen shore,

By mortal eye ne'er seen before,

To you, good-morrow.

Cosmo Monkhouse from "To a New-Born Child"

It is better that the mother discover her child by touching it.
Better to feel before she sees. Better to sense this warm and trembling life,
to be moved in her heart by what her *hands* tell her.
To hold her child rather than merely look at it.

Frederick Leboyer *Birth Without Violence*

If all is dim and quiet, warm and peaceful, the baby will relax after his
traumatic journey. His breathing will steady. His crumpled face will smooth
itself out and his eyes will open. His head will lift a little and his limbs
will move against your skin. Put very gently to your bare breast, he may suck,
discover a new form of human contact and feel a little less separated. These
are his first contacts with his new world: let him make them without distress.
These are his first moments of life; let him have them in peace.

Penelope Leach *Your Baby & Child*

Whenever a child is born
All night a soft wind rocks the corn;
One more buttercup wakes to the morn,
Somewhere, Somewhere.

Agnes Carter Mason from "Somewhere"

A baby is God's opinion that the world should continue.

Anonymous

A recent story tells about a baby who was giggling and laughing minutes
after he was born. The obstetrician noticed he had unusual
muscle control, his tiny left fist being tightly clenched.
When the doctor pried it open, he found a contraceptive pill.

Evan Esar *The Comic Encyclopedia*

I believe that each newborn child arrives on earth
with a message to deliver to mankind. Clenched in his little fist is
some particle of yet unrevealed truth, some missing clue,
which may solve the enigma of man's destiny.
He has a limited amount of time to fulfill his mission
and he will never get a second chance—nor will we.
He may be our last hope. He must be treated as top sacred.

In a cosmos in which all things appear to have a meaning, what is *his* meaning?
We who are older and presumably wiser must find the key to unlock
the secret he carries within himself. The lock cannot be forced.
Our mission is to exercise the kind of loving care which will prompt
the child to open his fist and offer up his truth, his individuality,
the irreducible atom of his self. We must provide the kind of environment in which
the child will joyfully deliver his message through complete self-fulfillment.

Sam Levenson *Everything but Money*

Every child is born a genius.

R. Buckminster Fuller

Every child is an artist.
The problem is how to remain an artist when he grows up.

Pablo Picasso

The greatness of the human personality begins at the hour of birth.
From this almost mystic affirmation there comes what may seem
a strange conclusion: that education must start from birth.

Maria Montessori *The Absorbent Mind*

Talk of Columbus and Newton! I tell you the child just born in yonder
hovel is the beginning of a revolution as great as theirs.
But you must have the believing and prophetic eye.

Ralph Waldo Emerson from "Education"

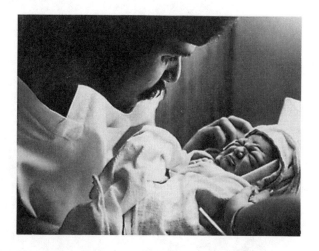

The aged-looking little face suddenly
puckered up still more and the baby sneezed.

Smiling, hardly able to restrain tears, Levin kissed his wife and went
out of the dark room. What he felt toward this little creature
was utterly unlike what he had expected.
There was nothing cheerful or joyous in the feeling;
on the contrary, it was a new torture of apprehension.
It was the consciousness of a new sphere of liability to pain.
And this sense was so painful at first, the apprehension
lest this helpless creature should suffer so intense,
that it prevented him from noticing the strange thrill
of senseless joy and even pride that he had felt when the baby sneezed.

Leo Tolstoy *Anna Karenina*

The joys of parents are secret, and so are their griefs and fears.

Francis Bacon from "Of Parents and Children"

If one but realized it, with the onset of the first pangs of birth pains,
one begins to say farewell to one's baby.
For no sooner has it entered the world,
when others begin to demand their share. With the child
at one's breast, one keeps the warmth of possession a little longer.

Princess Grace of Monaco

How delicate the skin, how sweet the breath of children!

Euripides, *Medea*

A little child born yesterday,
A thing on mother's milk and kisses fed.

Homer from "Hymn to Hermes"

In the sheltered simplicity of the first days after a baby is born,
one sees again the magical closed circle,
the miraculous sense of two people existing only for each other,
the tranquil sky reflected on the face of the mother nursing her child.

Anne Morrow Lindbergh *Gift from the Sea*

I saw his eyes open full to mine,

and realized each of us was fastened to the other,

not only by mouth and breast, but through our mutual gaze:

the depth, calm, passion, of that dark blue, maturely focused look.

Adrienne Rich *Of Woman Born*

My day-old son is plenty scrawny,

His mouth is wide with screams, or yawny,

His ears seem larger than his needing.

His nose is flat, his chin receding,

His skin is very, very red,

He has no hair upon his head,

And yet I'm proud as proud can be

To hear you say he looks like me.

Richard Armour "Miniature"

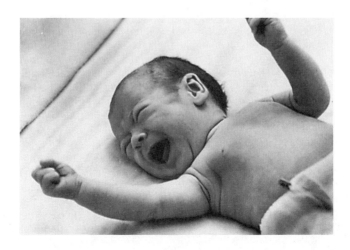

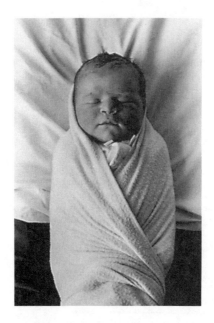

Sweetest l'il' feller, everybody knows;

Dunno what to call him, but he's mighty lak'

a rose.

Frank L. Stanton from "Mighty Lak' a Rose"

"I have no name;

"I am but two days old."

What shall I call thee?

"I happy am,

Joy is my name."

Sweet joy befall thee!

William Blake from "Infant Joy"

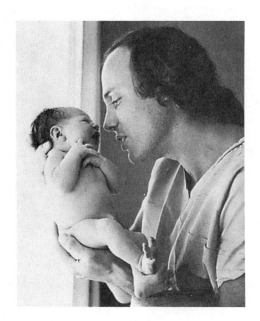

There came to port last Sunday night
  The queerest little craft,
Without an inch of rigging on;
  I looked and looked—and laughed.
It seemed so curious that she
  Should cross the unknown water,
And moor herself within my room—
  My daughter! O my daughter!

George W. Cable from "The New Arrival"

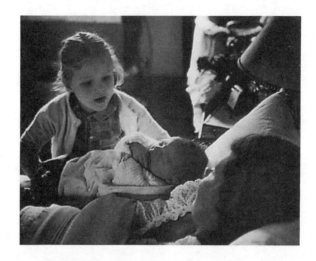

I have got a new-born sister;
I was nigh the first that kissed her.
When the nursing woman brought her
To papa, his infant daughter,
How papa's dear eyes did glisten!—
She will shortly be to christen:
And papa has made the offer,
I shall have the naming of her.

Now I wonder what would please her,
Charlotte, Julia, or Louisa.
Ann and Mary, they're too common;
Joan's too formal for a woman;
Jane's a prettier name beside;
But we had a Jane that died.
They would say, if 'twas Rebecca,
That she was a little Quaker.

Edith's pretty, but that looks
Better in old English books;
Ellen's left off long ago;
Blanche is out of fashion now.
None that I have named as yet
Are so good as Margaret.
Emily is neat and fine.
What do you think of Caroline?
How I'm puzzled and perplexed
What to choose or think of next!
I am in a little fever,
Lest the name that I shall give her
Should disgrace her or defame her,
I will leave papa to name her.

Charles and Mary Lamb "Choosing a Name"

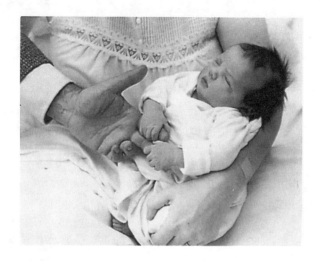

There is only one child in the world
and the child's name is All Children.

Carl Sandburg from the "Prologue" to *The Family of Man*

I must confess, I felt something special when I carried
him for the circumcision. The circumcision is a very mystical rite.
The rabbi had a very beautiful way of putting it.
He said, "A name has returned." A name has returned.

Elie Weisel

HOMECOMING

A babe in a house is a well-spring of pleasure.

Martin Farquhar Tupper from "Of Education"

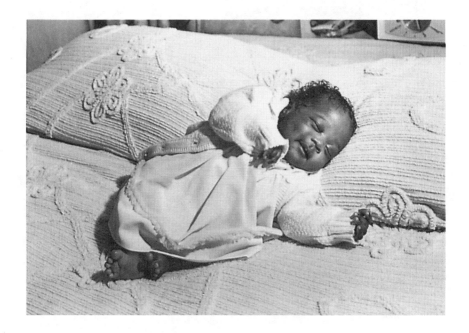

Then there had been the inspection of their child from head to toe as he

watched Annie undress the baby before bedtime. The tiny perfect

fingernails and toenails astonished him the most.

They were like the small pink shells you scuffed

up on the sands of tropical beaches, he whispered, counting them.

And for the twentieth time, he exclaimed,

"I don't know how you did it all alone!" His admiration for her bravery

sent a glow of happiness through her. It was a new kind of tribute from him.

It was payment in full for the terrors of her lonely ordeal.

Bessie Breuer *Annie's Captain*

The two-year-old has had a motherless week. Mother has gone

   to bring back the baby. A week is many many years.

   One evening they bring the news to the playpen: a

   child is born, you have a baby brother. The dark little

   eyes consider this news and convey no message. One

   day long after, they arrive in a taxi, father, mother,

   bundle. The two-year-old observes from her blue

   walker on the sunny sidewalk. She stares and turns

   away on her wheels.

Karl Shapiro "The Two-Year-Old Has Had a Motherless Week"

Nobody asked *me* if I wanted a baby sister.

Martha Alexander from *Nobody Asked ME If I Wanted a Baby Sister*

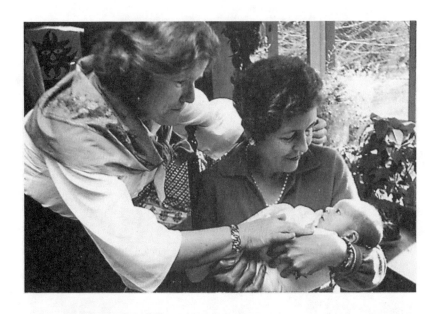

If you're having your first baby, make sure you get a grandmother
there as soon as possible. You may think you know all there
is to know about life, but you can't touch her when it comes to this. . . .

They made sounds that I can only describe as animal-like when
they saw her . . . it was as if something squeezed their hearts.
I realized that nothing I may ever accomplish in the world of work
will possibly affect them the way the sight of their granddaughter did.

Bob Greene *Good Morning, Merry Sunshine*

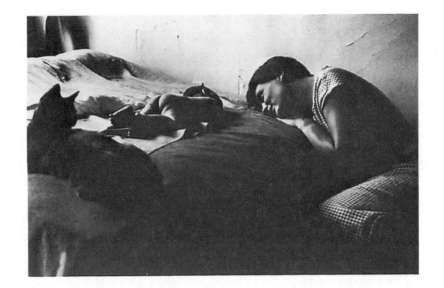

The cat

who purrs

so sweetly

cannot fathom

why her place

in our bed

has been taken

by this one

who cries.

Susan Eisenberg "The Baby"

During the first weeks, I used to lie long hours with the baby in my arms,
watching her asleep; sometimes catching a gaze from her eyes;
feeling very near the edge, the mystery, perhaps the knowledge of Life . . .

Isadora Duncan *My Life*

The sweetest flowers in all the world—
A baby's hands.

Algernon Charles Swinburne from "Étude Réaliste"

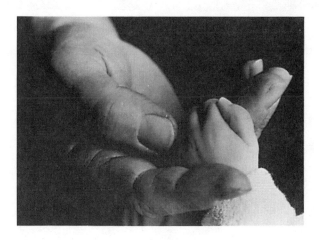

Rosefrail and fair — yet frailest
A wonder wild
In gentle eyes thou veilest,
My blueveined child.

James Joyce from "A Flower given to my Daughter"

Of the dark past
A child is born;
With joy and grief
My heart is torn.

Calm in his cradle
The living lies.
May love and mercy
Unclose his eyes!

James Joyce from "Ecce Puer"

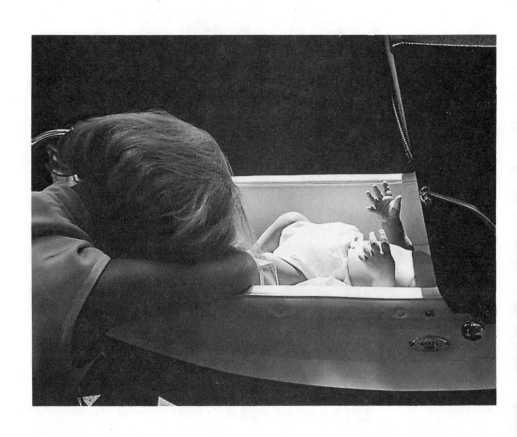

AMBIVALENCE

I looked down at that baby, and suddenly I felt that a
whole part of my life had just ended, been cut off,
and I was beginning something for which I had no preparation.

Bob Greene *Good Morning, Merry Sunshine*

I did not feel anything like the warm bond I was supposed to feel for this
bundle newly removed from my body. As far as I was concerned,
any relationship between that squirmy creature and my own bulging flesh
was purely coincidental. Over and over in my mind, I kept thinking that
getting close to your baby was like getting close to your mother-in-law:
everyone expects you to feel affection for a complete stranger.
That expectation burdens the relationship from the very beginning, though
I admit that babies have more going for them than a mother-in-law does.

Angela Barron McBride *The Growth and Development of Mothers*

Becoming a father is easy enough,

But being one can be rough.

Wilhelm Busch *Julchen*

Paternity is a career imposed on you without any inquiry into your fitness.

Adlai E. Stevenson

Love set you going like a fat gold watch.
The midwife slapped your footsoles, and your bald cry
Took its place among the elements.

Our voices echo, magnifying your arrival. New statue.
In a drafty museum, your nakedness
Shadows our safety. We stand round blankly as walls.

I'm no more your mother
Than the cloud that distils a mirror to reflect its own slow
Effacement at the wind's hand.

All night your moth-breath
Flickers among the flat pink roses. I wake to listen:
A far sea moves in my ear.

One cry, and I stumble from bed, cow-heavy and floral
In my Victorian nightgown.
Your mouth opens clean as a cat's. The window square

Whitens and swallows its dull stars. And now you try
Your handful of notes;
The clear vowels rise like balloons.

Sylvia Plath "Morning Song"

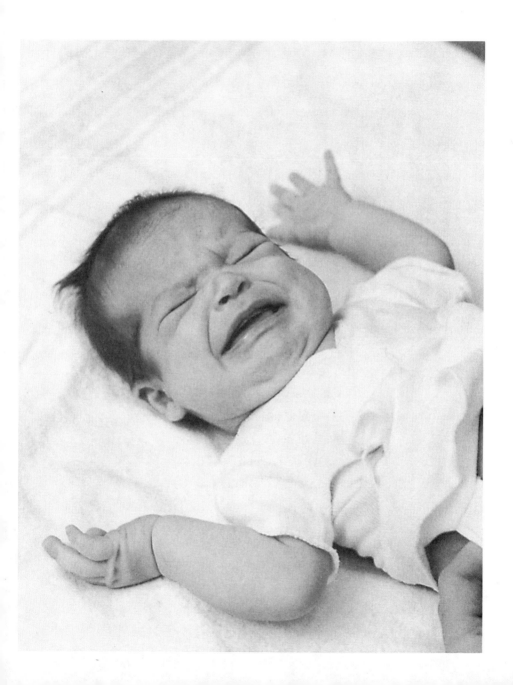

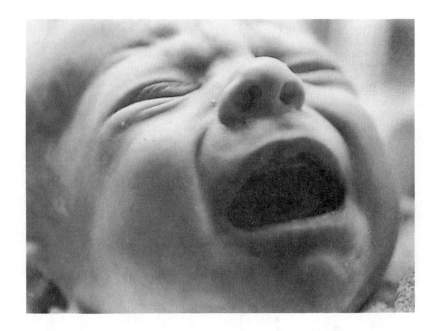

Can a mother sit and hear

An infant groan, an infant fear?

No, no! never can it be!

Never, never can it be!

William Blake "On Another's Sorrow"

An infant crying in the night:

An infant crying for the light:

And with no language but a cry.

Alfred Lord Tennyson from "In Memoriam, A.H.H."

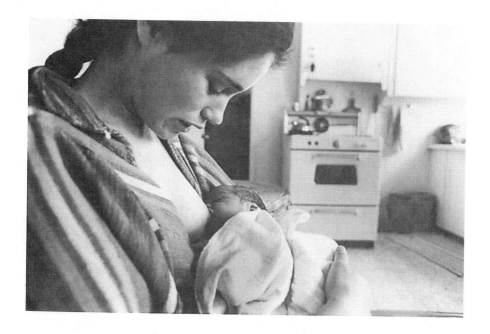

They were connected through her breasts. Every few hours Ariane
cried for her, every few hours her breasts ached to be suckled.
They were bound in animal linkage and that bond was the most real
thing she could still feel. But she was frightened.
She did not feel that she loved her baby. This strange animal
in her lap with its smells and loud cries, the fierce desires
that shook it, she was not quite sure what she was doing with it.

Marge Piercy *Small Changes*

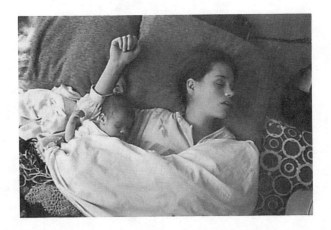

Who was this immensely powerful person,

screaming unintelligibly, sucking my breast until I

was in a state of fatigue the likes of which I had never known?

Who was he and by what authority had he claimed the right to my life?

Jane Lazarre *The Mother Knot*

Tonight I see how scared I am. There is so much to do for this little creature

who screams and wriggles and needs and doesn't know what he needs

and relies on me to figure it all out. I watch myself run away, leaving the baby

to Susan and her woman's intuition and her breasts full of milk.

David Steinberg *Fatherjournal*

Dreading the cry, longing for the cry,
the young mother leads what is called
her own life
while the baby sleeps.

Sharon Olds from "Young Mothers V"

We need love's tender lessons taught
   As only weakness can;
God hath his small interpreters;
   The child must teach the man.

John Greenleaf Whittier from "Child-Songs"

O young thing, your mother's lovely armful!
How sweet the fragrance of your body!

Euripides

Hold a baby to your ear
    As you would a shell:
Sounds of centuries you hear
    New centuries foretell.

Who can break a baby's code?
    And which is the older—
The listener or his small load?
    The held or the holder?

E.B. White "Conch"

Our little bud of Paradise
Is wakeful, father. I suppose
His clever brain already knows
That if he bubbles long enough
His head will lean against the rough
Attraction of your overcoat.

Norman Gale

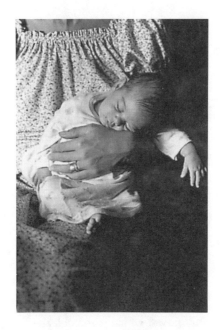

Oh mother,

here in your lap,

as good as a bowlful of clouds,

I your greedy child

am given your breast,

the sea wrapped in skin,

and your arms,

roots covered with moss

and with new shoots sticking out

to tickle the laugh out of me.

Yes, I am wedded to my teddy

but he has the smell of you

as well as the smell of me.

Your necklace that I finger
is all angel eyes.
Your rings that sparkle
are like the moon on the pond.
Your legs that bounce me up and down,
your dear nylon-covered legs,
are the horses I will ride
into eternity.

Oh mother,
after this lap of childhood
I will never go forth
into the big people's world
as an alien,
a fabrication,
or falter
when someone else
is as empty as a shoe.

Anne Sexton "Mothers"

It still wasn't the kind of love we had expected, the kind celebrated through the
centuries. It was the kind of love that made you feel as if your day began when
they went to sleep, but which also made you tiptoe into the bedroom
at least five times a night just to make sure they were still breathing.

Roberta Israeloff *Coming to Terms*

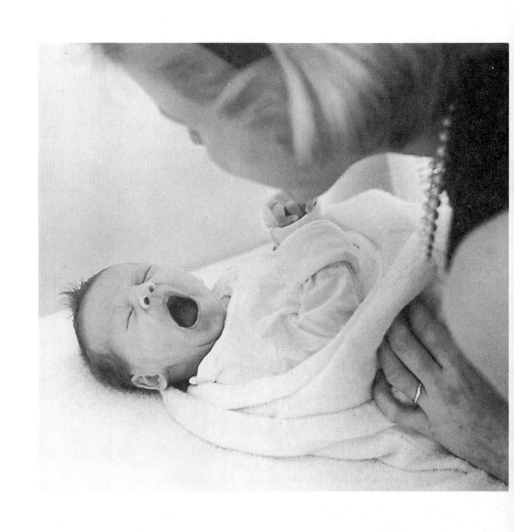

BEFORE DAWN

Now the moon is full again
& you are four weeks old.
Little lion, lioness,
yowling for my breasts,
growling at the moon,
how I love your lustiness,
your red face demanding,
your hungry mouth howling,
your screams, your cries
which all spell life
in large letters
the color of blood.

Erica Jong from "On the First Night"

. . . he co-operates
With a universe of large and noisy feeling-states
   Without troubling to place
Them anywhere special, for, to his eyes, Funnyface
   Or Elephant as yet
Mean nothing. His distinction between Me and Us
Is a matter of taste; his seasons are dry and wet;
He thinks as his mouth does.

W.H. Auden from "Mundus et Infans"

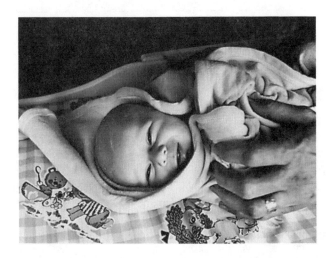

"What are you thinking about? Come on and tell us!"
The blurry baby eyes rest briefly on the face bending over it,
a ghost of a smile appears, then the ancient
tiny face grows blank and inscrutable,
silent as the Sphinx to its supplicants.

Selma H. Fraiberg *The Magic Years*

Some, admiring what motives to mirth infants meet with in their silent and
solitary smiles, have resolved . . . that then they converse with angels!

Thomas Fuller A *Pisgah-Sight of Palestine*

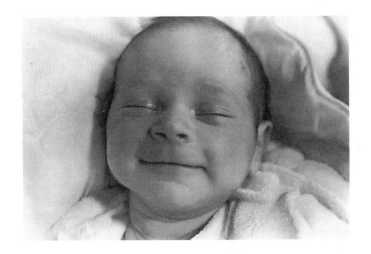

Babies receive signals from outer space,
bringing messages from other galaxies that only babies can detect.
These messages cause the baby to smile (if the message is a joke)
or look startled (if it is bad news, such as the explosion of a popular star).

Dave Barry *Babies & Other Hazards of Sex*

At six weeks Baby grinned a grin
That spread from mouth to eyes to chin,
And Doc, the smarty, had the brass
To tell me it was only gas!

Margaret Fishback from "Look Who's A Mother"

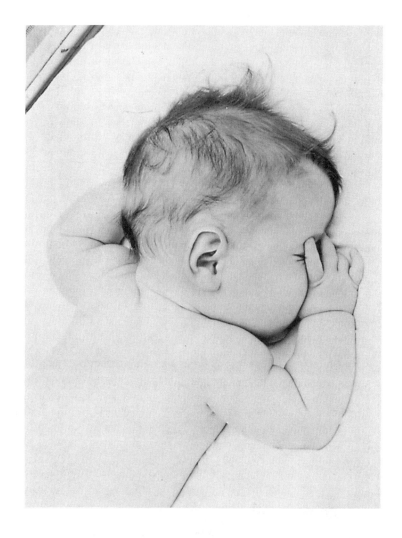

He smiles, and sleeps!—sleep on

And smile, thou little, young inheritor

Of a world scarce less young: sleep on and smile!

George Gordon, Lord Byron from "Cain"

And underneath the pram cover lies my brother Jake

He is not old enough yet to be properly awake

He is alone in his sleep; no arrangement they make

For him can touch him at all, he is alone,

For a little while yet, it is as if he had not been born

Rest in infancy, brother Jake; childhood and interruption come

swiftly on.

Stevie Smith "Childhood and Interruption"

CARE AND FEEDING

My God, the human baby! A few weeks after birth, any other animal
can fend for itself. But *you*! A basket case till you're twenty-one.

Megan Terry *The Magic Realist*

Defenseless as babies are, they have mothers at their command,
families to protect the mothers, societies to support the structure of families,
and traditions to give a cultural continuity to systems of tending and training.

Erik H. Erikson *Insight and Responsibility*

The baby came. A boy. Just like I said.

They called him Benjamin.

I called him AWFUL.

At first all he did was sleep, eat, and spit up.

All they did was spend every second with HIM.

"Not now," they said. They were feeding the baby.

Or diapering him. Or burping him. Or cleaning

   his spit up. Or putting him to sleep.

Patricia Lakin *Don't Touch My Room*

Babies are not the helpless, innocent creatures they appear to be.
Beneath that wrinkled, rosy exterior lurk the mind and instincts
of a seasoned guerrilla fighter, determined to force you, the parent,
into unconditional surrender. No holds barred, no weapon too ghastly
to be used against you. Predawn attacks are commonplace;
assaults with loaded diapers and ear-piercing battle cries
are just the beginning of the struggle.

But what is the war about? What does the little monster want?
Just this: your total and unquestioning obedience to every
gurgle and yell; the rearrangement of your entire life to suit his or her schedule;
and twenty-four-hour attention. During the first year, your baby
will try to lay the foundations for a whole childhood of making you jump.

Peter Mayle *Baby Taming*

The decision to eat strained lamb or not to eat strained lamb should be
with the "feedee" not the "feeder." Blowing strained lamb into the
feeder's face should be accepted as an opinion, not as a declaration of war.

Erma Bombeck *If Life is a Bowl of Cherries—What Am I Doing in the Pits?*

My baby cries—and All the world is
wrong.
My baby laughs—The world is full of
song.

Betel Nuts or What They Say in Hindustan

This is the Basic Baby Mood Cycle,

which all babies settle into once they get over being born:

MOOD ONE: Just about to cry

MOOD TWO: Crying

MOOD THREE: Just finished crying

Your major job is to keep your baby in Mood Three as much as possible.
Here is the traditional way to do this. When the baby starts to cry,
the two of you should pass it back and forth repeatedly and recite
these words in unison: "Do you suppose he's hungry? He can't be hungry.
He just ate. Maybe he needs to be burped. No, that's not it.
Maybe his diaper needs to be changed. No, it's dry.
What could be wrong? Do you think he's hungry?"
And so on, until the baby can't stand it anymore and decides to go to sleep.

Dave Barry *Babies & Other Hazards of Sex*

Today, it's as much a part of a baby's face as his nose or ears,
but thirty years ago the pacifier was considered a maternal crutch,
a visual that screamed to the world "I can't cope."

I was a closet pacifier advocate. So were most of my friends.
Unknown to our mothers, we owned thirty or forty of those
little suckers that were placed strategically around the house
so a cry could be silenced in less than thirty seconds.
Even though bottles were boiled, rooms disinfected,
and germs fought one on one,
no one seemed to care where the pacifier had been.

Erma Bombeck, *Motherhood The Second Oldest Profession*

A soiled baby, with a neglected nose,
cannot be conscientiously regarded as a thing of beauty.

Mark Twain

There's only one pretty child in the world, and every mother has it.

Chesire Proverb

There is something about babyness that brings out the softness
in people and makes them want to hug and protect this small thing
that moves and dribbles and produces what we poetically call "poopoo."
Even *that* becomes precious, for the arrival of a baby
coincides with the departure of our minds. My wife and I often summoned
the grandparents of our first baby and proudly cried, "Look! Poopoo!"
A statement like this is the greatest single disproof of evolution I know.

Bill Cosby *Fatherhood*

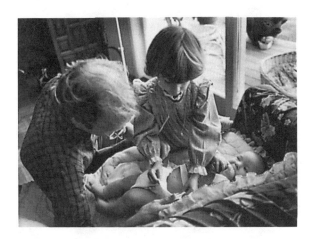

Happy is he who has no children;
for babies bring nothing but crying and stench.

Eustace Deschamps

Now first of all he means the night
    You beat the crib and cried
And brought me spinning out of bed
    To powder your backside.

I rolled your buttocks over
    And I could not complain:
Legs up, la la, legs down, la la,
    Back to sleep again.

James Wright from "A Song for the Middle of the Night"

I wouldn't mind so much
being your all-night cafe, if
after lingering over your drink
you politely went off to bed.

It's those nights when you
nurse one drink
and then order another
     looking so *offended*
       your lips in a tragic pout
when I suggest you've had enough

that make me consider
shutting the bar down altogether.

Susan Eisenberg "Breastfeeding at Night"

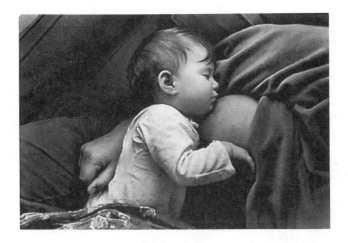

Kicking his mother until she let go of his soul

Has given him a healthy appetite: clearly her rôle

   In the New Order must be

To supply and deliver his raw materials free;

   Should there be any shortage,

She will be held responsible . . .

W.H. Auden from "Mundus et Infans"

Why do fairy tales always end with the prince and princess marrying?

Why don't they tell you what happened to the couple in the next fifty years.

How did the prince and princess feel when the babies started coming?

Did Cinderella ever wake up in the morning to the cry of her baby,

feeling as evil and fussy as her stepsisters?

Angela Barron McBride *The Growth and Development of Mothers*

Baby wakes up in the morning light
Pick her up and hold her tight.
Put little baby in the tub—
Scrubbity, scrubbity, scrub-scrub!
Squeeze the sponge and use the soap—
Baby's cool and clean (we hope!)
Dress her up in pretty clothes,
Then outside to play she goes.
Carry her, swing her, sing her a song—
We care for baby all day long!

Ernest Nister "Baby"

I have experienced agony, worry, boredom and intense irritation,
and I am writing to you as last time, on one hand shouting
"Whew! I've found a nurse!" and with the other hand mopping my brow.

Colette "Letters"

"Oh come on now," one nurse said. "You can't be *serious*." I'd asked her
whether the tapes on disposable diapers go in the back or front.
I wasn't born knowing how to type, either, I felt like telling her.
Why should I inherently know how to diaper?

Roberta Israeloff *Coming to Terms*

How to fold a diaper depends on the size of the baby and the size of the diaper.

Dr. Benjamin Spock *Baby & Child Care*

Cleaning your house while your kids are still growing
is like shoveling the walk before it stops snowing.

Phyllis Diller

"There's nothing to worry about" is a typical example of the kind of
easy-for-you-to-say remarks that pediatricians like to make.
Another one is, "Take his temperature rectally every hour,"
an instruction which, if actually followed,
would scar both parent and child emotionally for life.
If your baby has diaper rash, your pediatrician
may say, "Just leave the diaper off for a while."
This would be a wonderful idea if the baby would stop
shooting wastes out of its various orifices . . .

Dave Barry *Babies & Other Hazards of Sex*

You know, I still feel in my wrists certain echoes of the prampusher's knack,
such as, for example, the glib downward pressure one applied to the
handle in order to have the carriage tip up and climb the curb.

Vladimir Nabokov *Speak, Memory*

There is no more somber enemy of good art than the pram in the hall.

Cyril Connolly *Enemy of Promise*

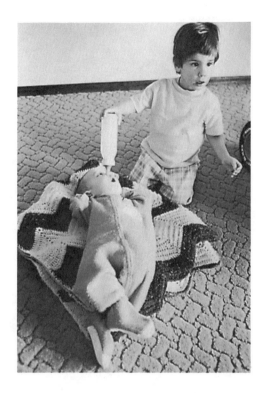

There is no finer investment for any community than putting milk into babies.

Winston Churchill

A man finds out what is meant by spitting image
when he tries to feed cereal to his infant.

Imogene Fey *Violets and Vitriol*

A child is fed with milk and praise.

Mary Lamb

There are one hundred and fifty-two distinctly different ways

of holding a baby—and all are right.

Heywood Broun *Seeing Things at Night*

I remember the quiet room, the dark
green chair where we sat afternoons,
the sun—no matter how tightly shuttered out—
coming in and curving across us
as if we were not separate, but a single body
joined in a ceremony of light.
My legs beneath you, my arms around you,
my breast under the glass bottle with rubber nipple,
I talked to you and sang to you,
No one interrupted us.
The dog sat quietly in the corner.
If I could have given birth to you,
I would have. I would have taken you
inside me, held you
and given birth to you again.
All the hours we spent in that room. Then,
one day, with your eyes focused on mine, you
reached up and stroked my cheek. Your touch
was that of the inchworm on its aerial thread
just resting on my skin, a larval curve
alighting and lifting off, a lightness
practicing for the time it will have wings.
I like to think wherever you go, you will
keep some memory of sunlight in the room
where I first loved you, and you first loved.

Fran Castan "The Adoption"

A W A K E N I N G

Begin, baby boy, to recognize your mother with a smile.

Virgil from "Eclogue 60"

When you're drawing up your list of life's miracles,
you might place near the top the first moment your baby smiles at you.

Bob Greene *Good Morning, Merry Sunshine*

heartcake   heartcake

   sweetened with breastmilk

   rising with kisses

the whole house

warmed by the fragrance

            of your smile

Susan Eisenberg "Simon"

What power there is in the smile of a child, in its play,

in its crying—in short, in its mere existence.

Are you able to resist its demand? Or do you hold out to it,

as a mother, your breast, or, as a father, whatever it needs of your belongings?

Max Stirner *Ego & His Own*

It is the physical weakness of a baby that makes it seem 'innocent,'

not the quality of its inner life.

St. Augustine *Confessions*

Sweet Babe, in thy face
Soft desires I can trace
Secret joys & secret smiles
Little pretty infant wiles.

As the softest limbs I feel
Smiles as of the morning steal
O'er thy cheek & o'er thy breast
Where thy little heart dost rest.

O, the cunning wiles that creep
In thy little heart asleep
When thy little heart does wake,
Then the dreadful lightnings
break.

From thy cheek & from thy eye
O'er the youthful harvests nigh
Infant wiles & infant smiles
Heaven & Earth of peace beguiles.

William Blake "A Cradle Song"

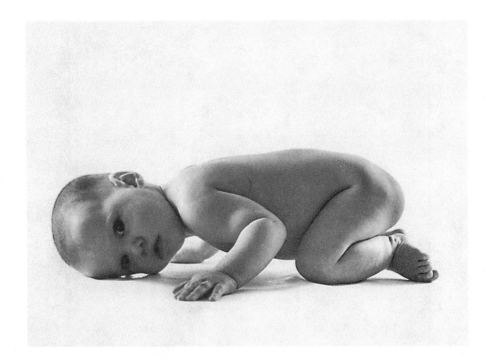

. . . when she's on her stomach she presses against the bottom
of the crib with her hands, and she grunts,
and it looks like she's trying to do push-ups. I wonder what's going on
inside her head, to make her feel she has to flip over to her back.
Everything in the world is done for her; this is the first and last time in her life
that she doesn't have to try to do anything. And yet every time I look at her,
she is struggling to turn. All I can think of
is that it's the beginning of ambition.

Bob Greene *Good Morning, Merry Sunshine*

Tender are a mother's dreams,

But her babe's not what he seems.

See him plotting in his mind

To grow up some other kind.

Clarence Day "Thoughts Without Words"

His greatness weigh'd, his will is not his own;
For he himself is subject to his birth:
He may not, as unvalued persons do,
Carve for himself; for on his choice depends
The safety and the health of this whole state.

William Shakespeare *Hamlet*

Among the three or four million cradles now rocking in the land
are some which this nation would preserve for ages as sacred things,
if we could know which ones they are.

Mark Twain Answering a toast "To the Babies"

The two-month-old baby has hardly roused himself
from the long night of his first weeks in this world
when he is confronted with some of the most profound problems of the race.
We invite him to study the nature of reality, to differentiate
between inner and outer experience, to discriminate self
and not-self and to establish useful criteria for each of these categories . . .

Selma H. Fraiberg *The Magic Years*

The Baby new to earth and sky,
What time his tender palm is prest
Against the circle of the breast,
Has never thought that 'this is I;'

But as he grows he gathers much,
And learns the use of 'I' and 'me'
And finds 'I am not what I see,
And other than the things I touch.'

Alfred Lord Tennyson from "In Memoriam A.H.H."

I placed Ben's head on my knees, his body stretched out along my thighs, and lifted his head to mine, taking a quick catch breath before saying "Benjamin" and dropping him back down. After a few rounds he stared into my eyes, waiting for me to begin again. He had caught on. A synapse in his brain hooked up; I could virtually hear it click into place as his belly laugh subsided. He wanted to laugh again. Our game was illuminated by his brilliant new awareness. He knew we were playing a game, he knew what would happen next, he knew who I was, and he knew that I knew that he knew. . . . That's all it took. A tiny door opened and I could see beyond it to all the possible pleasures in store. He had stolen my heart. It was spring at last and I was in love.

Roberta Israeloff *Coming to Terms*

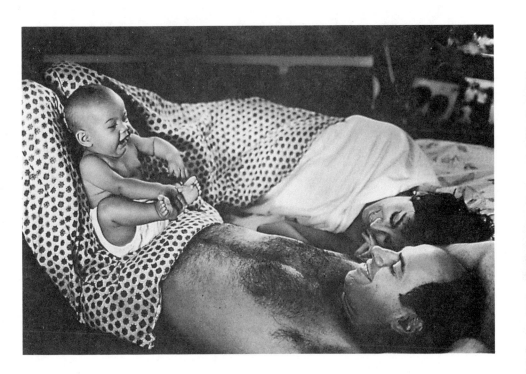

When the first baby laughed for the first time, the laugh broke into a thousand pieces and they all went skipping about, and that was the beginning of fairies.

J.M. Barrie *Peter Pan*

It occurs to me that the closest reproduction of the mind's birth obtainable is the stab of wonder that accompanies the precise moment when, gazing at a tangle of twigs and leaves, one suddenly realizes that what had seemed a natural component of that tangle is a marvelously disguised insect or bird.

Vladimir Nabokov *Speak, Memory*

The new-born child changes from day to day—
and the progress is observed in all of these
trifles, when the child is being bathed,
when it wakes from sleep, when it smiles for the first time,
and when the first glimmer of consciousness lightens in its eyes—
in every moment, in every note of its voice, it reveals itself anew.

The Plough Women: Memoirs of the Pioneer Women of Palestine

SENSORY
PLEASURES

She was a beautiful baby. She blew shining bubbles of sound.

She loved motion, loved light, loved color and music and textures.

She would lie on the floor in her blue overalls patting the surface so hard in

ecstasy her hands and feet would blur. She was a miracle to me. . . .

Tillie Olson from "I Stand Here Ironing"

Behold the child, by nature's kindly law

Pleas'd with a rattle, tickled with a straw.

Alexander Pope from "An Essay on Man"

Life in all its phases possessed for him unsounded depths of entertainment.

Josephine Dodge Bacon *The Memoirs of a Baby*

The child is a little inspector when it crawls

It touches and tastes the earth

Rolls and stumbles toward the object

Zigzags like a sail

And outmanuevers the room.

I am learning the child's way

I pick up wood pieces from the ground

And see shapes into them

I notice a purple velvet bee resting on a flower

And stop to listen to its buzz

They have included me

And though I will not be put away to rock alone

And don't roll down the plush hills

   Nor spit for lunch

   I am learning their way

They have given me back the bliss

    of my senses.

Hy Sobiloff from "The Child's Sight"

The world he discovers is a vast and intricate jig-saw puzzle,

thousands of pieces scrambled together in a crazy juxtaposition.

Piece by piece he assembles the fragments into whole objects and the objects

into groups until he emerges with a fairly coherent picture

of the tiny piece of world he inhabits . . .

This learning . . . is a prodigious intellectual feat.

No wonder every parent thinks his baby is a genius. He is!

And like all geniuses this baby works indefatigably at his discoveries.

He is intoxicated with his new-found world; he devours it with every

sense organ. He marvels at the bit of dust he picks up in his fingers.

A piece of cellophane, a scrap of foil,

a satin ribbon will fill him with rapture. He revels in the kitchen cupboards,

pursues the hidden treasures of drawers, waste-baskets and garbage cans.

This urge for discovery is like an insatiable hunger

that drives him on and on relentlessly. He is drunk with fatigue,

but he cannot stop. The hunger for sensory experience is as

intense and all-consuming as the belly hunger of the first months of life.

Selma H. Fraiberg *The Magic Years*

Only a mother's heart can be
Patient enough for such as he.

Ethel Lynn Beers from "Which Shall it Be?"

A curly, dimpled lunatic.

Ralph Waldo Emerson from "Nature"

Now having seduced him into the sensory pleasures of this world and caused
him to embrace it with his whole being, let us try to take it away from him and
put him back in darkness. Sleep? But look, he can't keep his eyes open!
He's drunk with fatigue. He howls with indignation at the extended hands,
rouses himself with mighty exertion from near collapse
to protest to these villains who take away his bright and beautiful world.
From his crib, in the darkened room he denounces these monster parents,
then pleads for commutation of sentence in eloquent noises.
He fights valiantly, begins to fail—then succumbs to his enemy, Sleep.

Selma H. Fraiberg *The Magic Years*

There never was a child so lovely but his mother was glad to get him asleep.

Ralph Waldo Emerson from "Journals"

You are my one, and I have not another:
Sleep soft, my darling, my trouble and
treasure;
Sleep warm and soft in the arms of your
mother,
Dreaming of pretty things, dreaming of
pleasure.

Christina G. Rossetti from "Little One Weary"

Over my slumbers your loving watch keep;
Rock me to sleep, mother; rock me to sleep.

Elizabeth Chase from "Rock Me to Sleep"

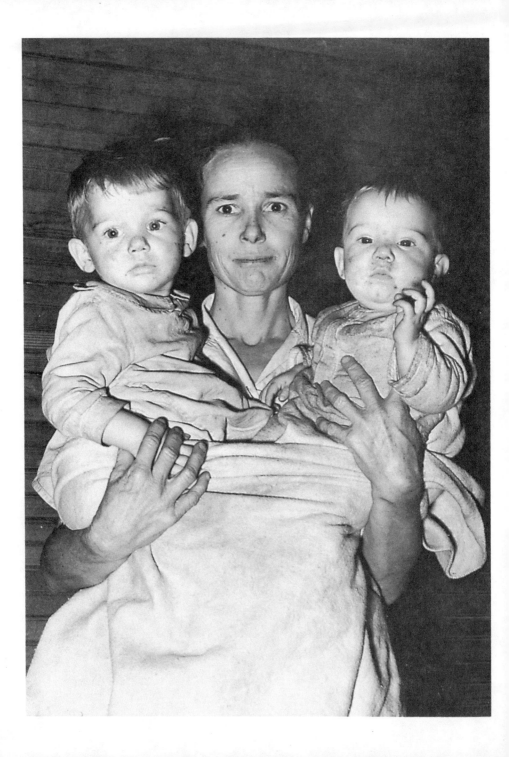

PARENTING

Infancy's the tender fountain,
Power may with beauty flow,
Mother's first to guide the streamlets,
From them souls unresting grow—
Grow on for the good or evil,
Sunshine streamed or evil hurled;
For the hand that rocks the cradle
Is the hand that rules the world.

William Ross Wallace from "The Hand that Rocks the Cradle is the Hand that Rules the World"

And often have I wondered

how the years and I survived.

I had a mother who sang to me

an honest lullaby.

Joan Baez from "Honest Lullaby"

The precursor of the mirror is the mother's face.

Donald Winnecott *Playing and Reality*

The mother's heart is the child's schoolroom.

Henry Ward Beecher *Life Thoughts*

Youth fades; love droops; the leaves of
friendship fall:
A mother's secret love outlives them all.

Oliver Wendell Holmes from "The Mother's Secret"

You kept them from harm.

That was what you did in the world if you were a mother.

Mary Gordon *Men and Angels*

O HUSH thee, my baby, thy sire was a knight,
Thy mother a lady, both lovely and bright;
The woods and the glens, from the towers which we see,
They all are belonging, dear baby, to thee.

O fear not the bugle, though loudly it blows,
It calls but the warders that guard thy repose;
Their bows would be bended, their blades would be red,
Ere the step of a foeman drew near to thy bed.

O hush thee, my baby, the time soon will come,
When thy sleep shall be broken by trumpet and drum;
Then hush thee, my darling, take rest while you may,
For strife comes with manhood, and waking with day.

Sir Walter Scott "Lullaby of an Infant Chief"

If there must be trouble let it be in my day, that my child may have peace.

Thomas Paine from "The American Crisis, I"

The time not to become a father is eighteen years before a war.

E.B. White *The Second Tree from the Corner*

See yon pale stripling! When a boy,
A mother's pride, a father's joy!

Sir Walter Scott from "Rokeby"

To be a successful father, there's one absolute rule:
when you have a kid, don't look at it for the first two years.

Ernest Hemingway

All babies look like Winston Churchill.

Anonymous

Th' expectant wee-things, toddlin', stacher through
   To meet their Dad, wi flichterin' noise an' glee.
His wee bit ingle, blinkin bonnilie,
   His clean hearth-stane, his thrifty wifie's smile,
The lisping infant prattling on his knee,
   Does a' his weary kiaugh and care beguile,
An' makes him quite forget his labour an' his toil.

Robert Burns from "The Cotter's Saturday Night"

Hush little baby,
don't say a word,
Daddy's gonna buy you
a mockingbird.
And if that mockingbird
won't sing,
Daddy's gonna buy you
a diamond ring.
And if that diamond ring
is brass,
Daddy's gonna buy you
a looking glass.
And if that looking glass
gets broke,
Daddy's gonna buy you
a billy goat.

And if that billy goat
won't pull,
Daddy's gonna buy you
a cart and bull.
And if that cart and bull
turn over,
Daddy's gonna buy you
a dog named Rover.
And if that dog named Rover
won't bark,
Daddy's gonna buy you
a horse and cart.
And if that horse and cart
fall down,
You'll still be the sweetest
little baby in town.

Traditional lullaby

Nothing is dearer to an old father than a daughter.

Sons have spirits of higher pitch, but they are not given to fondness.

Euripides *The Suppliant Woman*

Greatness of name in the father oft-times overwhelms the son;

they stand too near one another. The shadow kills the growth: so much,

that we see the grandchild come more and oftener to be heir of the first.

Ben Jonson *Timber; or, Discoveries Made Upon Men and Matter*

It is no new observation, I believe, that a lover in most cases
has no rival so much to be feared as the father.

Charles Lamb "The Wedding"

. . . I never see an infant (male),

A- sleeping in the sun,

Without I turn a trifle pale.

And think is *he* the one . . .

. . . Oh, somewhere he bubbles bubbles of milk,

And quietly sucks his thumbs.

His cheeks are roses painted on silk,

And his teeth are tucked in his gums.

But alas, the teeth will begin to grow,

The bubbles will cease to bubble;

Given a score of years or so,

The roses will turn to stubble.

He'll sell a bond, or he'll write a book,

And his eyes will get that acquisitive look,

And raging and ravenous for the kill,

He'll boldly ask for the hand of Jill.

This infant whose middle

Is diapered still

Will want to marry

My daughter Jill . . .

Ogden Nash from "Song to be Sung by the Father of Infant Female Children"

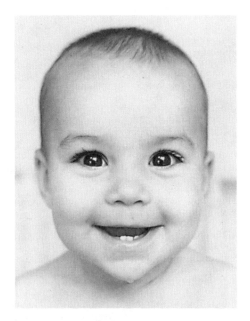

The magician is seated in his high chair and looks upon the world with favor.

He is at the height of his powers. If he closes

his eyes, he causes the world to disappear.

If he opens his eyes, he causes the world to come back.

If there is harmony within him, the world is harmonious.

If rage shatters his inner harmony, the unity of the world is shattered.

If desire arises within him, he utters the magic

syllables that cause the desired object to appear.

His wishes, his thoughts, his gestures, his noises command the universe.

Selma H. Fraiberg *The Magic Years*

Adam and Eve had many advantages,
but the principal one was that they escaped teething.

Mark Twain *Pudd'nhead Wilson*

Through the house what busy joy,

Just because the infant boy

Has a tiny tooth to show!

I have got a double row,

All as white, and all as small;

Yet no one cares for mine at all.

He can say but half a word,

Yet that single sound's preferred

To all the words that I can say

In the longest summer day.

He cannot walk, yet if he put

With mimic motion out his foot,

As if he thought he were advancing.

It's prized more than my best dancing.

Charles and Mary Lamb "The First Tooth"

Infancy conforms to nobody; all conform to it.

Ralph Waldo Emerson from "Self-Reliance"

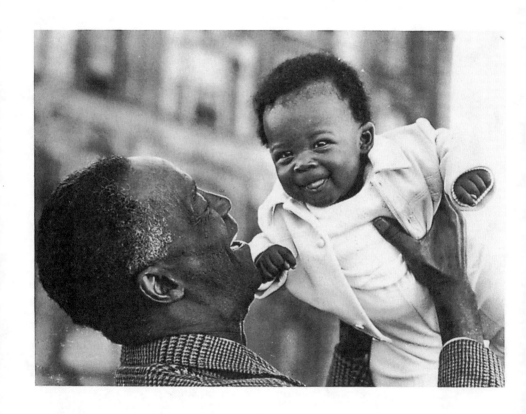

GRANDPARENTING

The best babysitters, of course, are the baby's grandparents.
You feel completely comfortable entrusting your baby
to them for long periods, which is why most grandparents
flee to Florida at the earliest opportunity.

Dave Barry *Babies & Other Hazards of Sex*

The children had'em. Let them raise'em.
That's what kills so many elderly women—raising grandchildren.

Moms Mabley

At six o'clock in the evening,
  The time for lullabies,
My son lay on my mother's lap
  With sleepy, sleepy eyes!
(O drowsy little manny boy,
  With sleepy, sleepy eyes!)

I heard her sing and rock him,
  And the creak of the swaying chair,
And the old dear cadence of the words
  Came softly down the stair.

And all the years had vanished,
  All folly, greed and stain—
The old, old song, the creaking chair,
  The dearest arms again!
(O lucky little manny boy,
  To feel those arms again!)

Christopher Morley

We haven't all had the good fortune to be ladies;

we haven't all been generals or poets, or statesmen;

but when the toast works down to the babies, we stand on common ground.

Mark Twain Answering a toast "To the Babies"

Babies haven't any hair;

Old men's heads are just as bare;

Between the cradle and the grave

Lies a haircut and a shave.

Samuel Hoffenstein from "Songs of Faith in the Year after Next"

As of the green leaves on a thick tree, some fall,
and some grow; so is the generation of flesh and blood,
one cometh to an end, and another is born.

Ecclesiasticus

. . . babies from generation to generation keeping
the Family of Man alive and continuing.

Carl Sandburg, from the "Prologue" to *The Family of Man*

A MIND
OF ONE'S OWN

For the first six months or so, your opponent has been confined to
areas of your choosing and has been unable to escape. Alas, the rules are
about to change drastically. . . . The enemy is now mobile . . .

If you feel you can't seal off the living room, you can disarm
the coffee table to a certain extent by clearing off the top completely
and by taping foam rubber padding round the sharp edges and corners.
This style is known as Infant Provincial . . .

Peter Mayle *Baby Taming*

❧

Babies do not want to hear about babies; they like to be told of giants and castles,
and of somewhat which can stretch and stimulate their little minds.

Samuel Johnson *Miscellanies*

❧

The illusions of childhood are necessary experiences. A child should not be
denied a balloon because an adult knows sooner or later it will burst.

Marcelene Cox *Ladies' Home Journal*

And a woman who held a babe against her bosom said, Speak to us of Children.

And he said:

Your children are not your children.

They are the sons and daughters of Life's longing for itself.

They come through you but not from you,

And though they are with you yet they belong not to you.

You may give them your love but not your thoughts,

For they have their own thoughts.

You may house their bodies but not their souls,

For their souls dwell in the house of tomorrow,

which you cannot visit, not even in your dreams.

You may strive to be like them, but seek not to make them like you.

For life goes not backward nor tarries with yesterday.

You are the bows from which your children as living arrows are sent forth.

The archer sees the mark upon the path of the infinite,

and He bends you with His might that His arrows may go swift and far.

Let your bending in the archer's hand be for gladness;

For even as He loves the arrow that flies,

so He loves also the bow that is stable.

Kahlil Gibran The Prophet

Families, when a child is born
Want it to be intelligent.
I, through intelligence
Having wrecked my whole life,
Only hope the baby will prove
ignorant and stupid.
Then he will crown a tranquil life
by becoming a Cabinet Minister.

Su Tung-P'O "On the Birth of his Son"

. . . each case was a person born, she was sure of it, with a nature more fixed
than modern thought led people to believe. She loved that, that her
children were not *tabulae rasae*, but had been born themselves.
She loved the intransigence of their natures, all that could never be molded
and so was free from her. . . . she respected the fixity of her children's souls
what they were born with, what she had, from the first months, seen.

Mary Gordon *Men and Angels*

We can't form our children on our own concepts;
we must take them and love them as God gives them to us.

Goethe *Hermann and Dorothea*

We were as twinn'd lambs that did frisk i' the sun,

And bleat the one at the other; what we chang'd

Was innocence for innocence; we knew not

The doctrine of ill-doing, nor dream'd

That any did.

William Shakespeare *The Winter's Tale*

When the baby gets born I see him, and he's full of life, or she is;

and I think to myself that it doesn't make any difference what

happens later, at least now we've got a chance, or the baby does.

You can see the little one grow and get larger and start doing things,

and you feel there must be some hope, some chance that things will get better;

because there it is, right before you, a real, live, growing baby.

Anonymous black woman *Children of Crisis*

It was life that would give her everything of consequence,

life would shape her, not we. All we were good for was to make

the introductions. We could introduce her to the sights and sounds and sensations.

How these reacted on her we must leave to her own private self.

It is hard to accept this background position, and like most parents,

we did not do it very well at all times. But we did at least understand our roles,

and that is a step toward a passing performance.

Helen Hayes *A Gift of Joy*

Nothing has a stronger influence psychologically on their environment,

and especially on their children, than the unlived life of the parents.

Carl Jung *Paracelsus*

Mature man needs to be needed, and maturity needs guidance as
well as encouragement from what has been produced and must be taken care of.

Erik H. Erikson *Childhood and Society*

The child is father of the man.

William Wordsworth from "My Heart Leaps Up"

I was realizing that babies brought more amplification than change; I
wasn't really different as much as more of myself...

Roberta Israeloff *Coming to Terms*

Man, a dunce uncouth,
Errs in age and youth:
Babies know the truth.

Algernon Charles Swinburne "Cradle Songs"

You—the purest pleasure
of my life,
the split pea
that proves
the ripeness of the fruit,
the unbroken center
of my broken hope—

O little one,
making you
has centered my lopsided life

So that if I know
a happiness
that reason never taught,

it is because of your small
unreasonably wrigglish
limbs.
Daughter, little bean,
sprout, sproutlet, smallest
girleen,
just saying your name
makes me grin.

I used to hate the word Mother,
found it obscene,
& now I love it
since that is me
to you.

Erica Jong "For Molly (A Verbal Cuddle for an Eight-month-old)"

VENTURING
FORTH

Thou straggler into loving arms,

Young climber up of knees,

When I forget thy thousand ways,

Then life and all shall cease.

Mary Anne Lamb from "A Child"

There is a thought that I have tried not to but cannot help
  but think,
Which is, My goodness how much infants resemble people
  who have had too much to drink.
Tots and sots, so different and yet so identical!
What a humiliating coincidence for pride parentical!
Yet when you see your little dumpling set sail across the
  nursery floor,
Can you conscientiously deny the resemblance to some-
  body who is leaving a tavern after having tried to
  leave it a dozen times and each time turned back for
  just one more?
Each step achieved
Is simply too good to be believed;
Foot somehow follows foot
And somehow manages to stay put;
Arms wildly semaphore,
Wild eyes seem to ask, Whatever did we get in such a
  dilemma for?
And their gait is more that of a duckling than a Greek
  goddessling or godling,
And in inebriates it's called staggering but in infants it's
  called toddling . . .

Ogden Nash from "It Must Be The Milk"

No flower-bells that expand and shrink

Gleam half so heavenly sweet,

As shine on life's untrodden brink

A baby's feet.

Algernon Charles Swinburne from "Étude Réaliste"

Only beginning the journey
Many a mile to go
Little feet, how they patter
Wandering to and fro

Trying again so bravely,
Laughing in baby glee;
Hiding its face in mother's lap
Proud as a baby can be

Tottering now and falling
Eyes that are going to cry
Kisses and plenty of love words
Willing again to try

George Cooper from "Learning to Walk"

There must be a solemn and terrible aloneness that comes over
the child as he takes those first independent steps. . . .
this moment must bring the first sharp sense of the uniqueness and separateness
of his body and his person, the discovery of the solitary self.

Selma H. Fraiberg *The Magic Years*

Father asked us what was God's noblest work.

Anna said *men*, but I said *babies*.

Men are often bad; babies never are.

Louisa May Alcott *Her Life, Letters and Journals*

May God Bless and keep you always

May your wishes all come true,

May you always do for others

And let others do for you.

May you build a ladder to the stars

And climb on every rung,

And may you stay forever young.

Bob Dylan from "Forever Young"

AFTERWORD

The sterilizer's up for grabs.

Nicked portacrib, good-bye.

My third and youngest son is growing older.

I'm done with dawn awakenings,

With Pablum in my eye,

With small moist bundles burping on my shoulder.

I gave away my drawstring slacks

And smocks with floppy bows.

My silhouette will never more be pear-ish.

And though I'm left with stretch marks

And a few veins varicose,

I'm aiming for an image less ma-mère-ish.

No playpens in the living room

Will mangle my décor.

My stairs will not be blocked with safety fences.

No rattles, bottles, bibs, stuffed bears

Will disarray my floor,

No eau de diaper pail assail my senses.

And no more babies will disrupt

The tenor of my day,

Nor croup and teething interrupt my sleeping.

I swear to you I wouldn't have it

Any other way.

It's positively stupid to be weeping.

Judith Viorst "No More Babies"

Grateful acknowledgment is made to the following for permission to reprint previously published material:

Atheneum Publishers, Inc. and The Sterling Lord Agency: excerpt from *Good Morning Merry Sunshine* by Bob Greene. Copyright © 1984 by John Deadline Enterprises, Inc. Reprinted with permission of Atheneum Publishers, Inc. and The Sterling Lord Agency.

Fran Castan: the poem "The Adoption" by Fran Castan. Copyright © 1986 by Fran Castan. First published in *Ms* magazine (June 1986). Reprinted by permission of the author.

Doubleday & Company, Inc.: excerpt from the poem "The Child's Sight" from *Breathing of First Things* by Hy Sobiloff. Copyright © 1963 by Hy Sobiloff. Reprinted by permission of Doubleday & Company, Inc.

Susan Eisenberg: two poems entitled "Breastfeeding at Night" and "Simon" by Susan Eisenberg. Copyright © 1986 by Susan Eisenberg; a poem entitled "The Baby" by Susan Eisenberg. Copyright © 1984 by Susan Eisenberg; and an excerpt from a poem entitled "Offerings" by Susan Eisenberg. Copyright © 1986 by Susan Eisenberg. Reprinted by permission.

Gabriel Earl Music: excerpts from the lyrics to "Honest Lullaby," lyrics by Joan Baez. Copyright © 1977, 1979 by Gabriel Earl Music.

Harper & Row Publishers, Inc.: a poem entitled "Conch" from *Poems and Sketches of E.B. White*. Copyright 1948 by E.B. White. Originally published in *The New Yorker*; a poem entitled "Morning Song" from *The Collected Poems of Sylvia Plath*, edited by Ted Hughes. Copyright © 1961, 1965, 1981 by Ted Hughes. World rights excluding the United States are administered by Olwyn Hughes Literary Agency. Reprinted by permission of Harper & Row Publishers, Inc. and Olwyn Hughes Literary Agency.

Henry Holt and Company, Inc. and The Sterling Lord Agency, Inc.: excerpt from "Playing with the Boys" from *Loveroot* by Erica Jong. Copyright © 1968, 1969, 1973, 1974, 1975 by Erica Mann Jong. Reprinted by permission of Henry Holt and Company, Inc. and The Sterling Lord Agency, Inc.

Alfred A. Knopf, Inc.: excerpt from "On Children" from *The Prophet* by Kahlil Gibran. Copyright 1923 by Kahlil Gibran and renewed 1951 by Administrators C.T.A. of the Kahlil Gibran Estate and Mary C. Gibran; excerpt from *Coming to Terms* by Roberta Israeloff. Copyright © 1982, 1984 by Roberta Israeloff. UK rights administered by Julian Bach Literary Agency, Inc. This title was published in the UK in the Pathway Series by Corgi Books, London; excerpt from *Your Baby and Child: From Birth to Age Five* by Penelope Leach. Copyright © 1977, 1978 by Dorling Kindersley Ltd., London. Text Copyright © 1977, 1978 by Penelope Leach. UK rights administered by Michael Joseph Ltd.; excerpt from "Thoughts without Words" from *The Best of Clarence Day*. Copyright 1928 by Clarence Day and renewed 1956 by Mrs. Clarence Day. Reprinted by permission.

Lescher & Lescher Ltd.: the poem "No More Babies" from *How Did I Get to Be 40 and Other Atrocities* by Judith Viorst, published by Simon & Schuster, Inc. Copyright © 1976 by Judith Viorst.

Little, Brown & Company: excerpt from *Children of Crisis: A Study of Courage and Fear* by Robert Coles. Copyright © 1964, 1965, 1966, 1967 by Robert Coles. Reprinted by permission of Little, Brown and Company in association with *The Atlantic Monthly Press*; excerpt from *Don't Touch My Room* by Patricia Lakin. Copyright © 1985 by Patricia Lakin Koenigsberg. UK rights administered by Blackie & Son Ltd., Glasgow and London; excerpt from "Pediatric Reflection" from *Family Reunion* by Ogden Nash. Copyright 1931 by Ogden Nash. UK and open market rights administered by Andre Deutsch Ltd.; excerpts from the poems "Song to be Sung by the Father of Infant Female Children," and "It Must be the Milk" from *I Wouldn't Have Missed It* by Ogden Nash. Copyright 1933, 1935 by Ogden Nash. First appeared in *The New Yorker*. UK and open market rights administered by Andre Deutsch Ltd. Reprinted by permission.

Liveright Publishing Corporation: excerpt form *A Treasury of Humorous Verse* by Samuel Hoffenstein. Copyright 1946 by Liveright Publishing Corporation. Copyright renewed 1974 by Liveright Publishing Corporation. Reprinted by permission of Liveright Publishing Corporation.

The Museum of Modern Art: excerpts from the prologue by Carl Sandburg to *The Family of Man*, edited by Edward